Abert's Squirrels

Reference Photos for Nature Artists

Photography and Text

By

Al Lodwick

DEDICATION

To Ann Lodwick, my wife and best friend, whose love and shared interests have supported me for almost 39 years.

INTRODUCTION

This is the eighth book in the Studies for Nature Artists Series. This series is designed for those artists who want to get every detail "just right". The people who use these reference photographs tell me that sometimes a less-than-perfect picture will still help them see how a subject holds its foot or some other body part. I have included some of these pictures, sacrificing perfect photography to show difficult details.

The pictures are grouped, as closely as possible, according to their posture. This arrangement makes it easy to switch back and forth when you are basing you work on more than one pose.

These pictures were mostly taken in the central Arizona highlands. Abert's Squirrels live almost exclusively in Ponderosa Pine woodlands. This is a transition zone between the cooler, wetter Ponderosa Pine and the hotter, dryer Oak-Pinyon-Juniper biomes. Consequently this population has access to a more varied diet than would animals of the same species living at higher elevations in a predominately Ponderosa Pine biome. It is acceptable to depict these animals as they appear in these pictures. Snow-capped peaks would be an unusual background for an Abert's Squirrel eating an acorn or climbing an Alligator Juniper tree.

Abert's (pronounced either A-bear or A-bert) Squirrels develop tassels on their ears during the colder months. If you choose to picture them in a snowy scene, the tassels should always be shown. In their habitat, snow does not cover all of the ground throughout the winter, so it is authentic to depict them on ground covered with pine needles or on tree branches with their tassels. If your work shows a summer scene, they should be shown without tassels.

I have taken literally thousands of photographs in Ponderosa Pine woodlands, so my previous books, *Acorn Woodpeckers, Bald Eagles, Cooper's Hawks, Double-crested Cormorants, Great Blue Herons, Snakes and Lizards*, and *Highlights of the Highlands Center and Lynx Lake Area of Arizona* also depict subjects in this habitat.

If you have any special needs for reference photos, please contact me at allodwick@gmail.com I have an extensive selection of photographs that are not, as yet, included in books.

Al Lodwick
Prescott, Arizona
July 2016

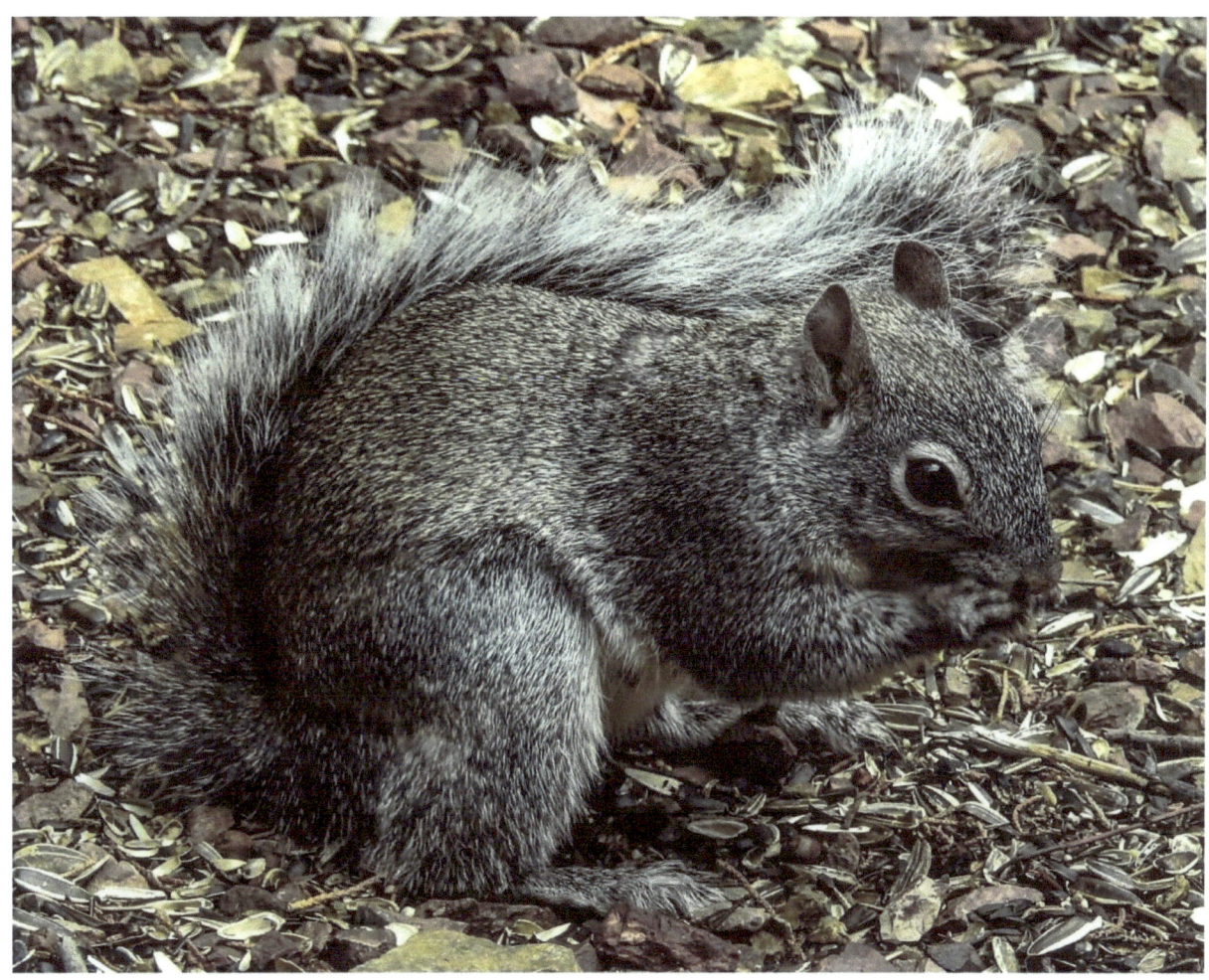

Abert's Squirrels spend a major portion of each day eating. This one was taken at a bird feeding station, so for a wild setting, do not show the sunflower seed hulls that are visible in this photograph. The tail over the back is a typical pose.

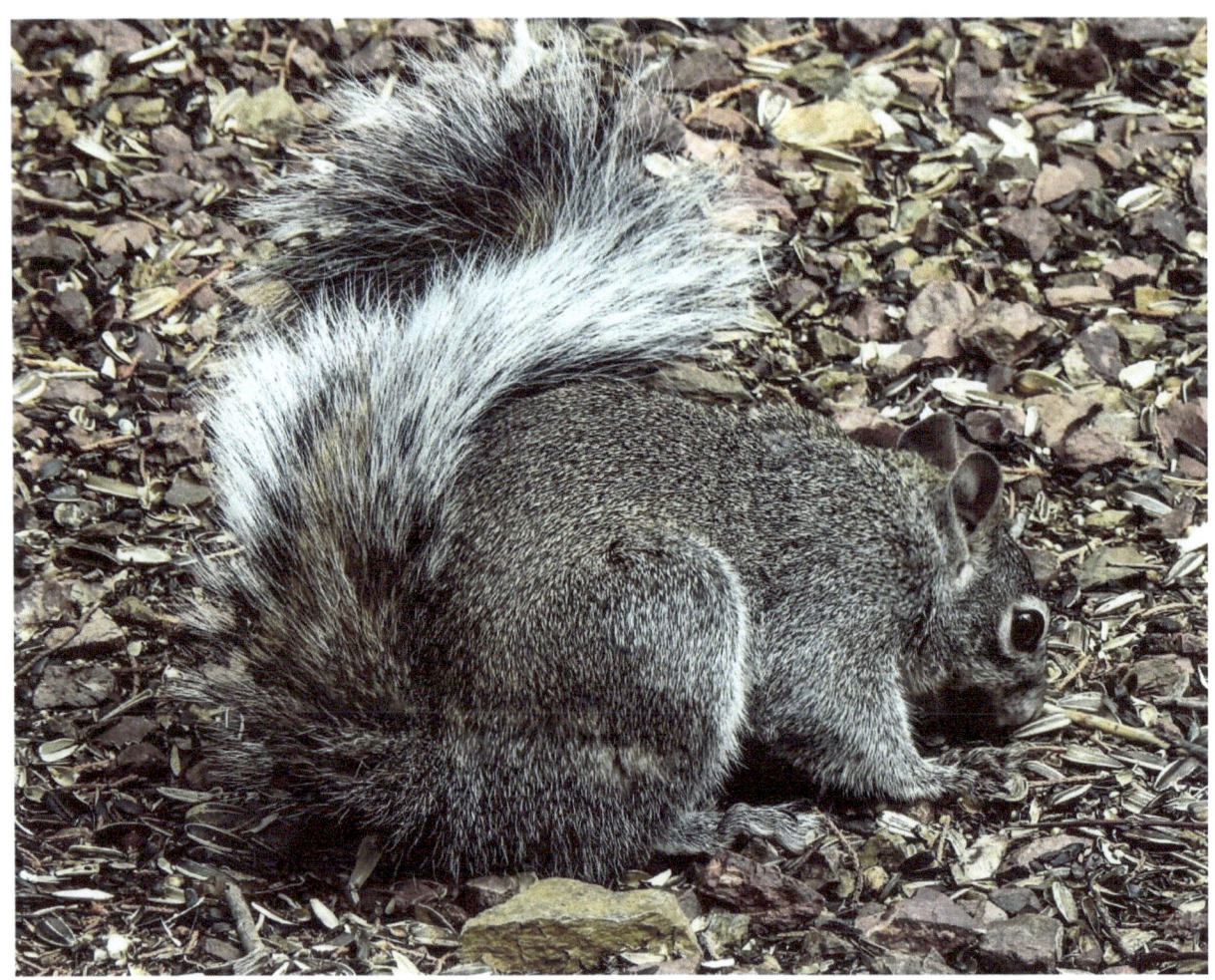

This picture was taken during August. At this time of year, Abert's Squirrels may not have ear tassels nor much rust color on their backs, as you will see on upcoming pages. Those will show more typical winter looks.

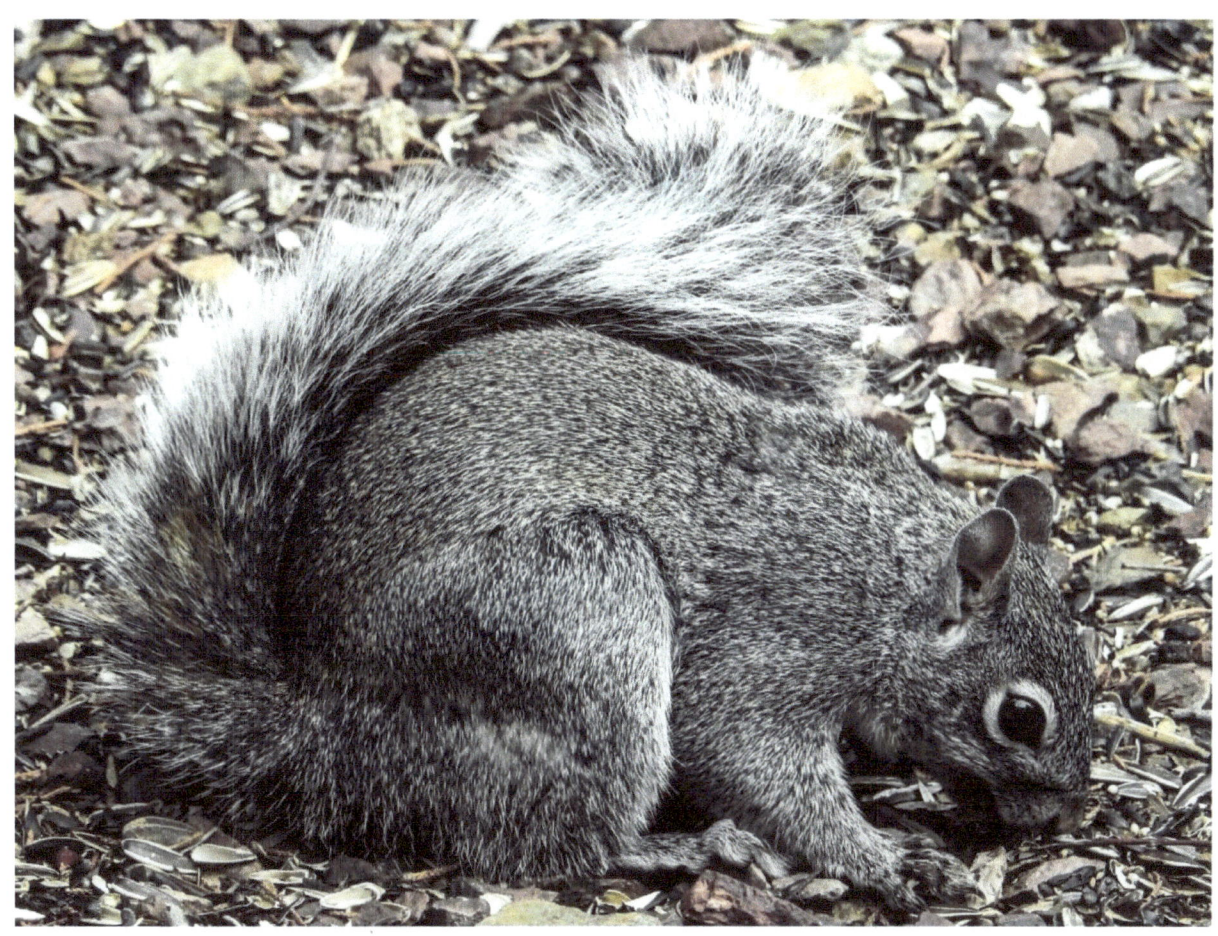

During the summer, Abert's Squirrels are forced to forage for just about anything they can eat. The Ponderosa Pine nuts that they prefer are not ripe yet, so they aren't very nutritious at this time of year,

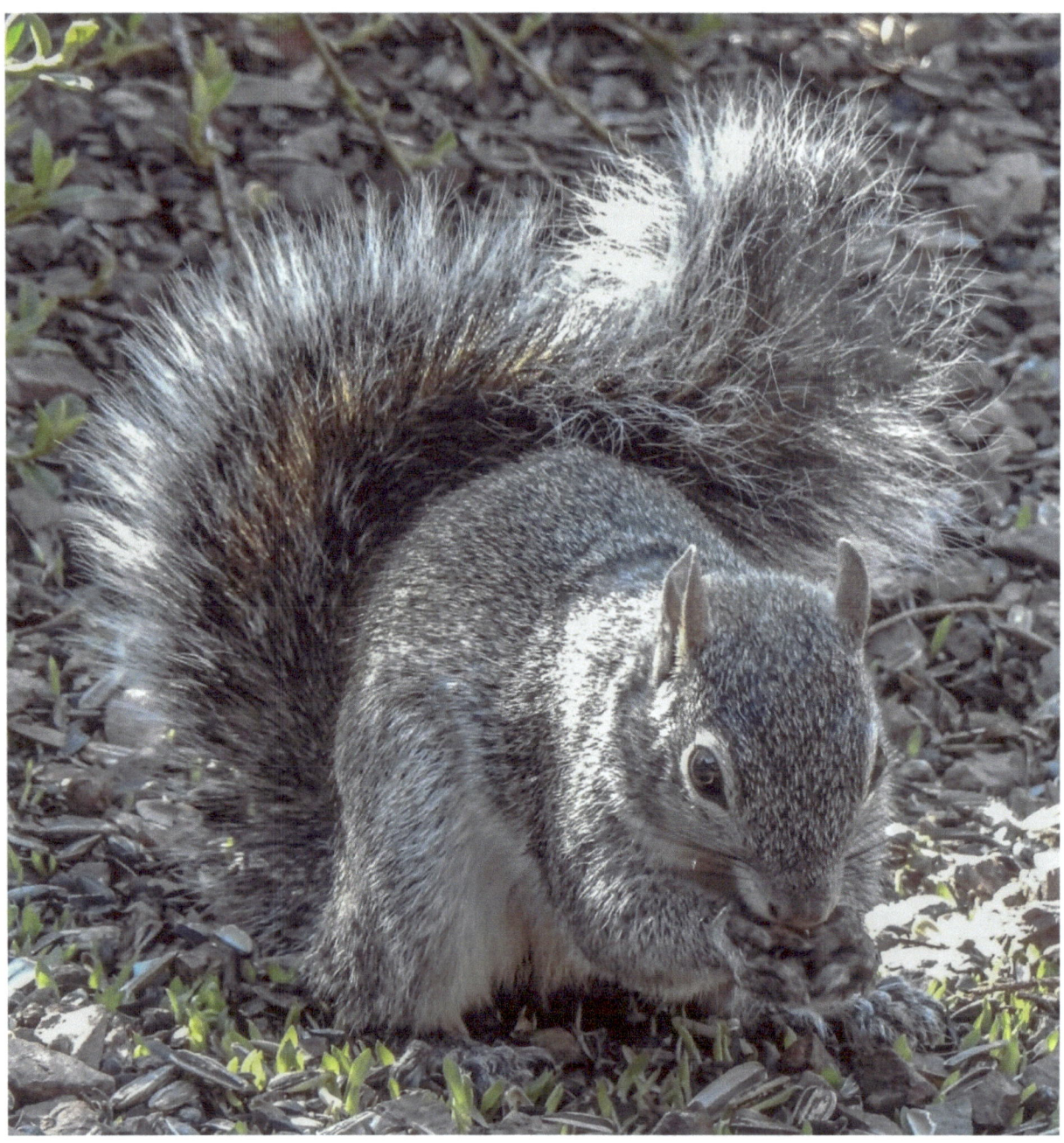

Look closely at the eyes in several photographs. You might choose to depict blue sky and a tall Ponderosa Pine reflected in the catch-light.

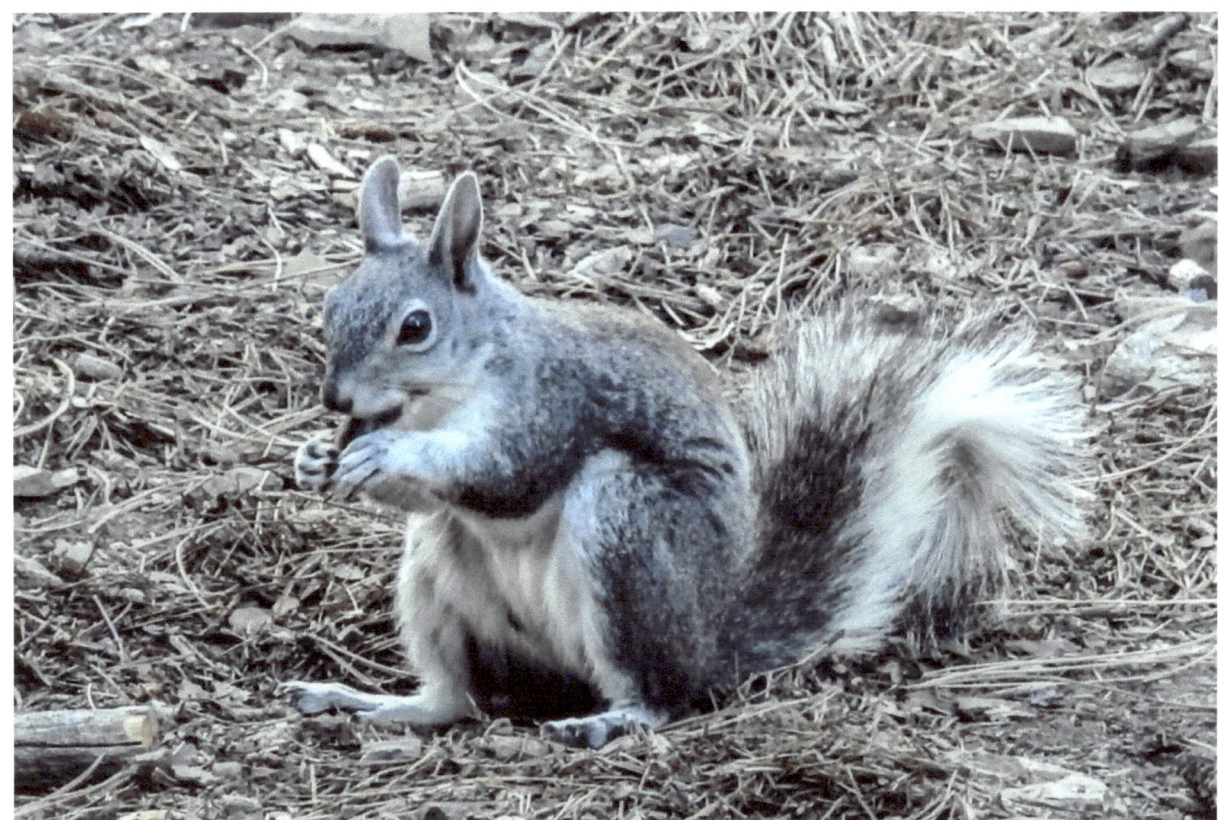

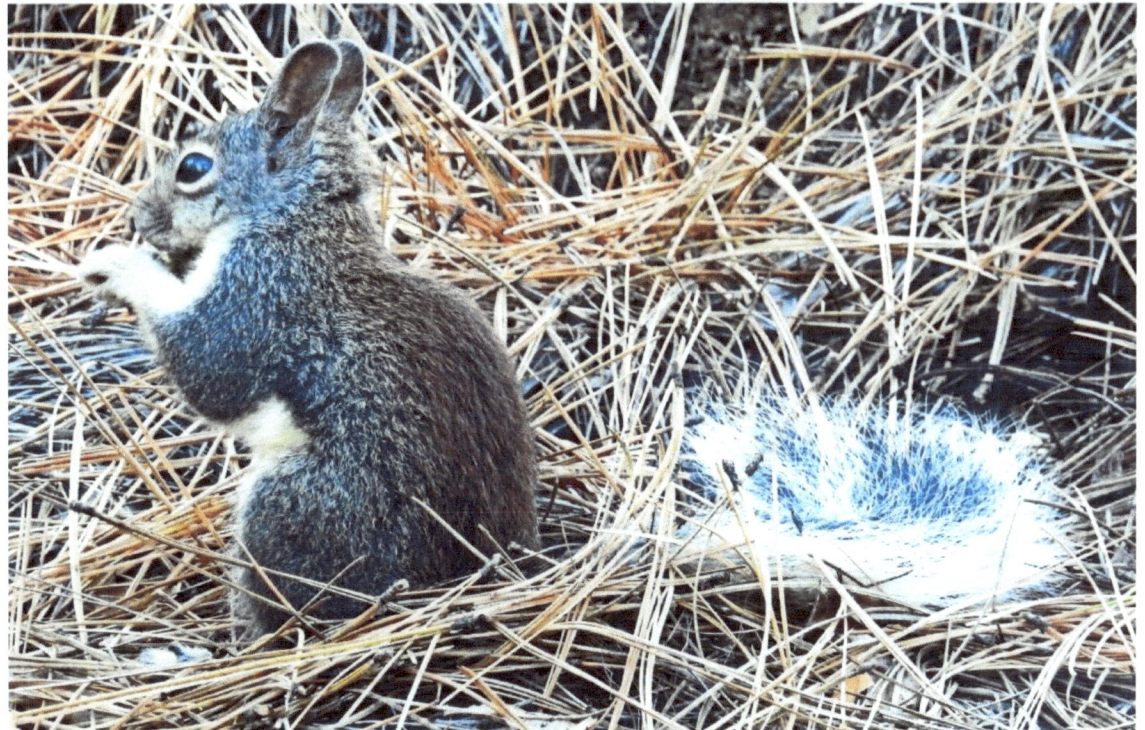

Ponderosa Pine needles are about 6" long and occur mostly in bundles of three.

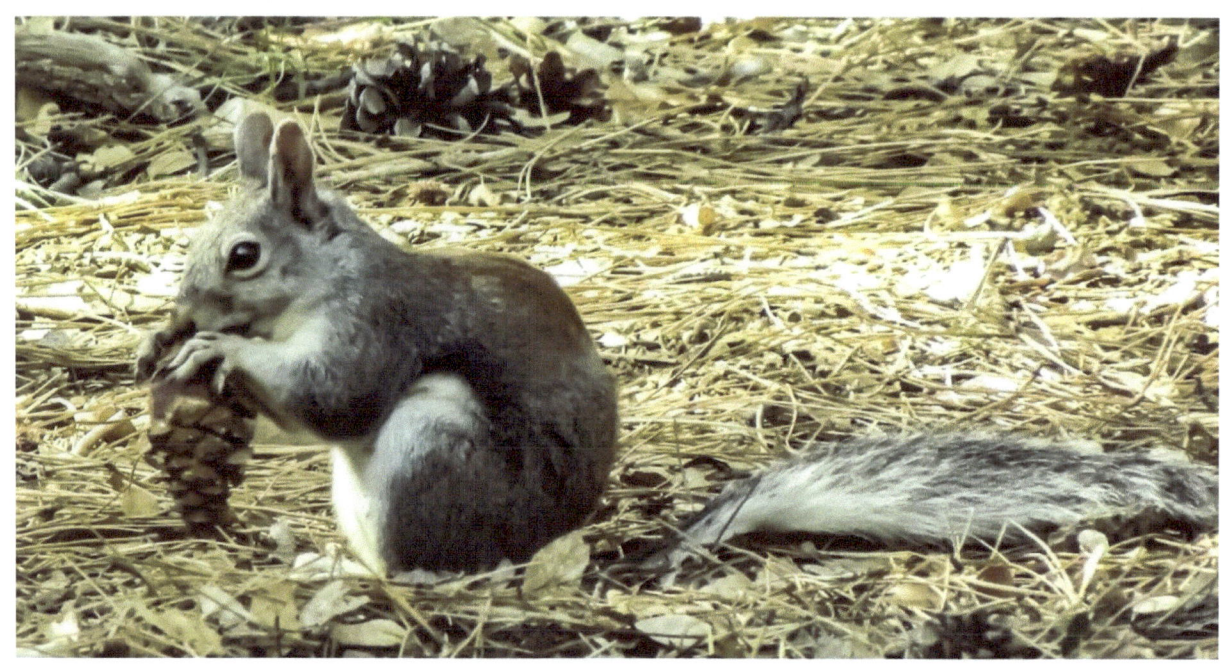

This picture illustrates how an Abert's Squirrel holds a Ponderosa Pine cone with its pointed end down to chew on it. In this way, it is able to gnaw away from the spiked ends on the cone.

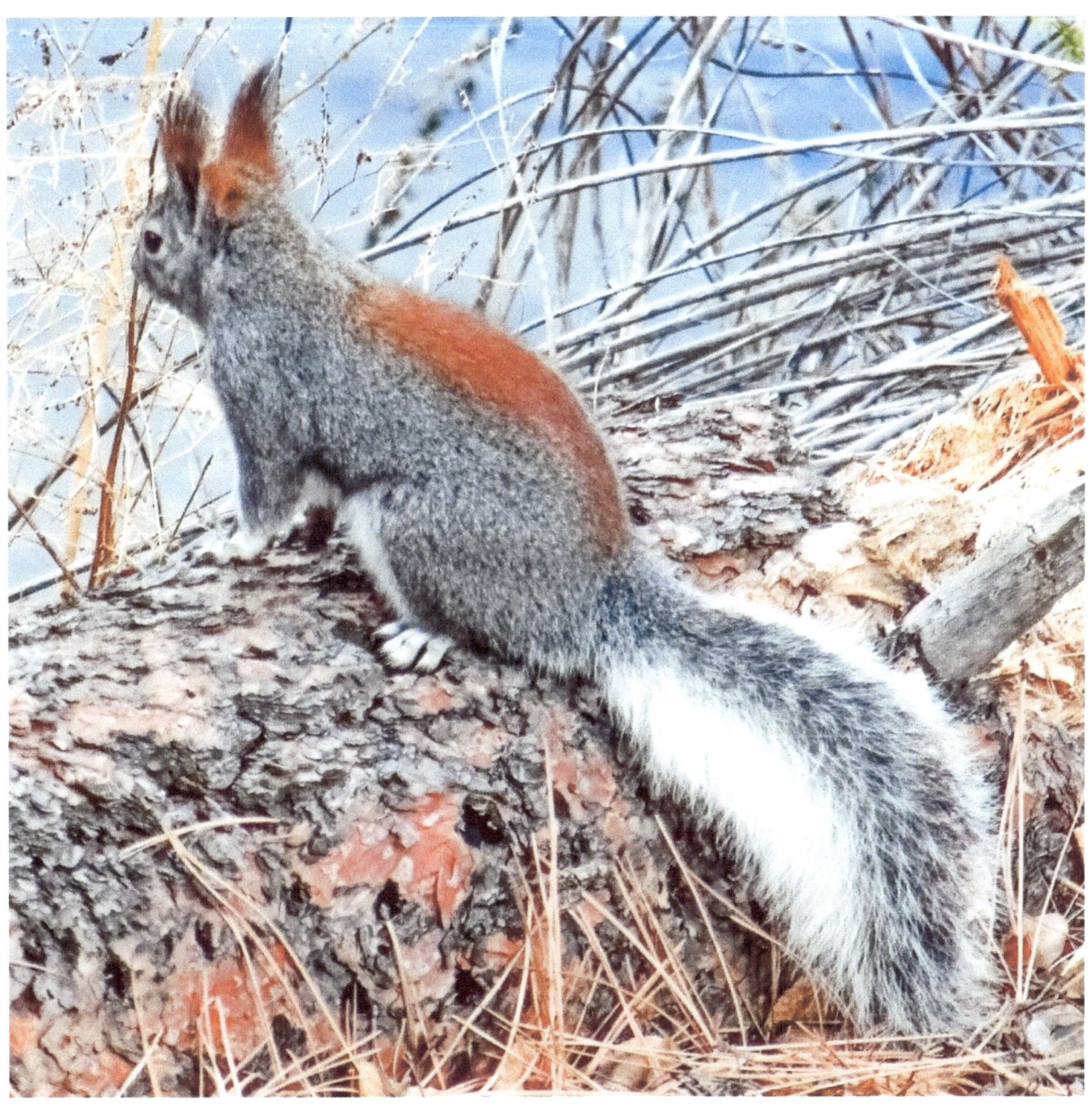

The red on this Abert's Squirrel's back and ears are a bit too bright. It should be closer to the shade of the pine needles and the bark on the fallen Ponderosa Pine trunk. This picture was taken in January, so it shows the extent of the winter coloring of the squirrel.

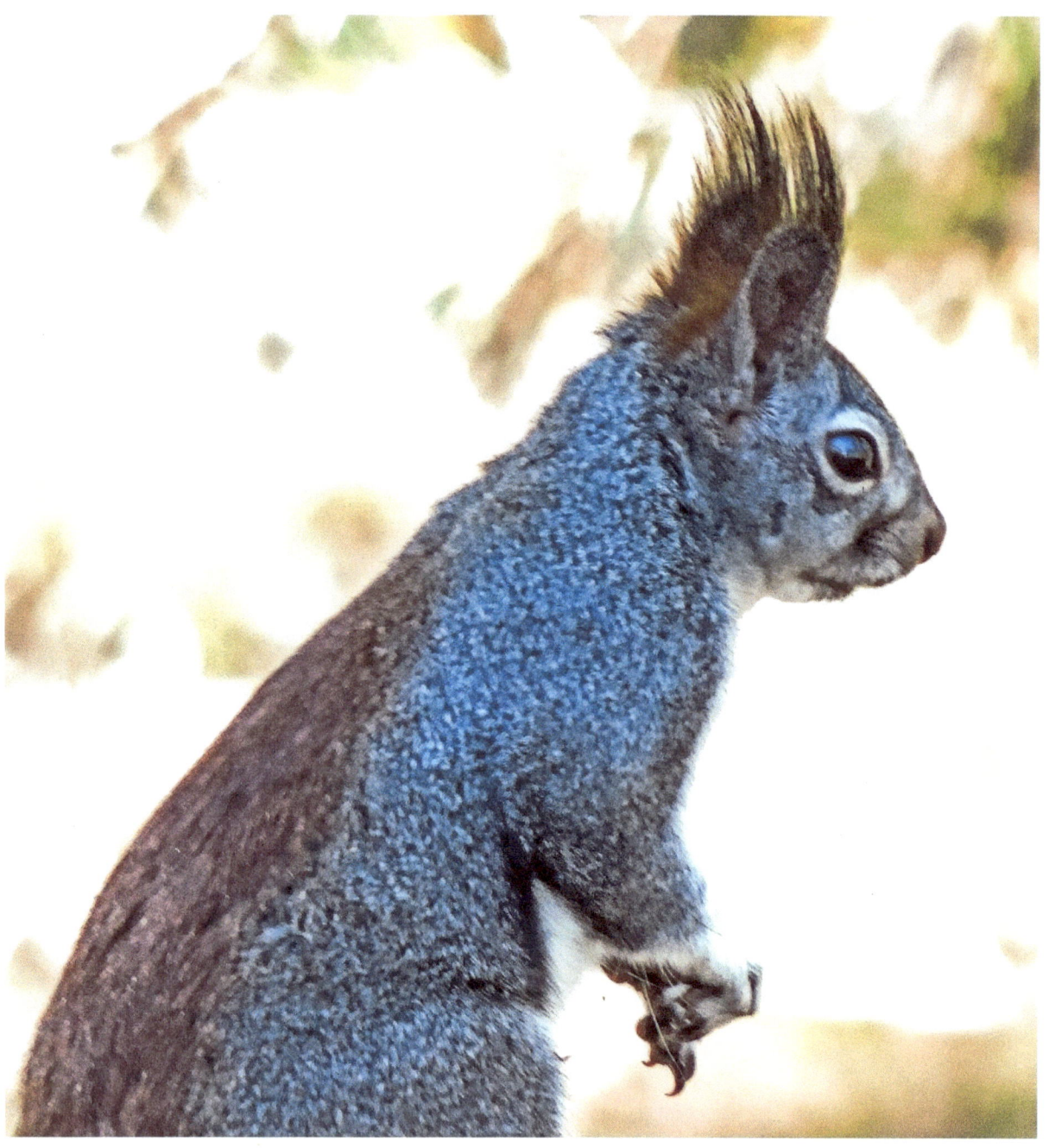

In this picture, the proper coloring of the Abert's Squirrel was sacrificed in order to show more details of the ear tassels. The picture on the previous page was a little too red and this one is too brown. Adjust your coloring to a shade between these two pictures.

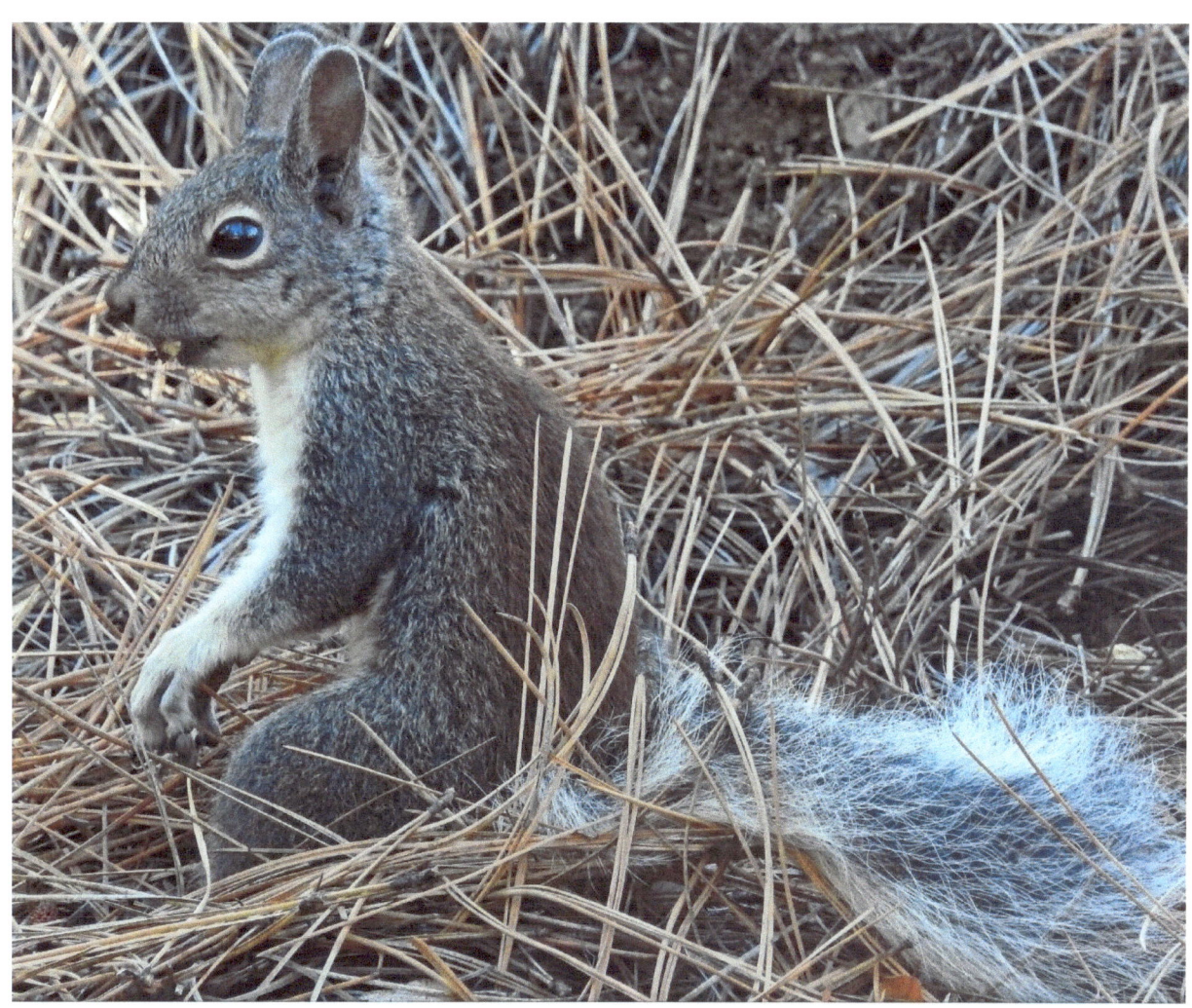

This Abert's Squirrel has spotted something approaching in the distance. Without 3-dimensional vision, it can be difficult to distinguish a dog from a coyote. It is probably assessing that threat.

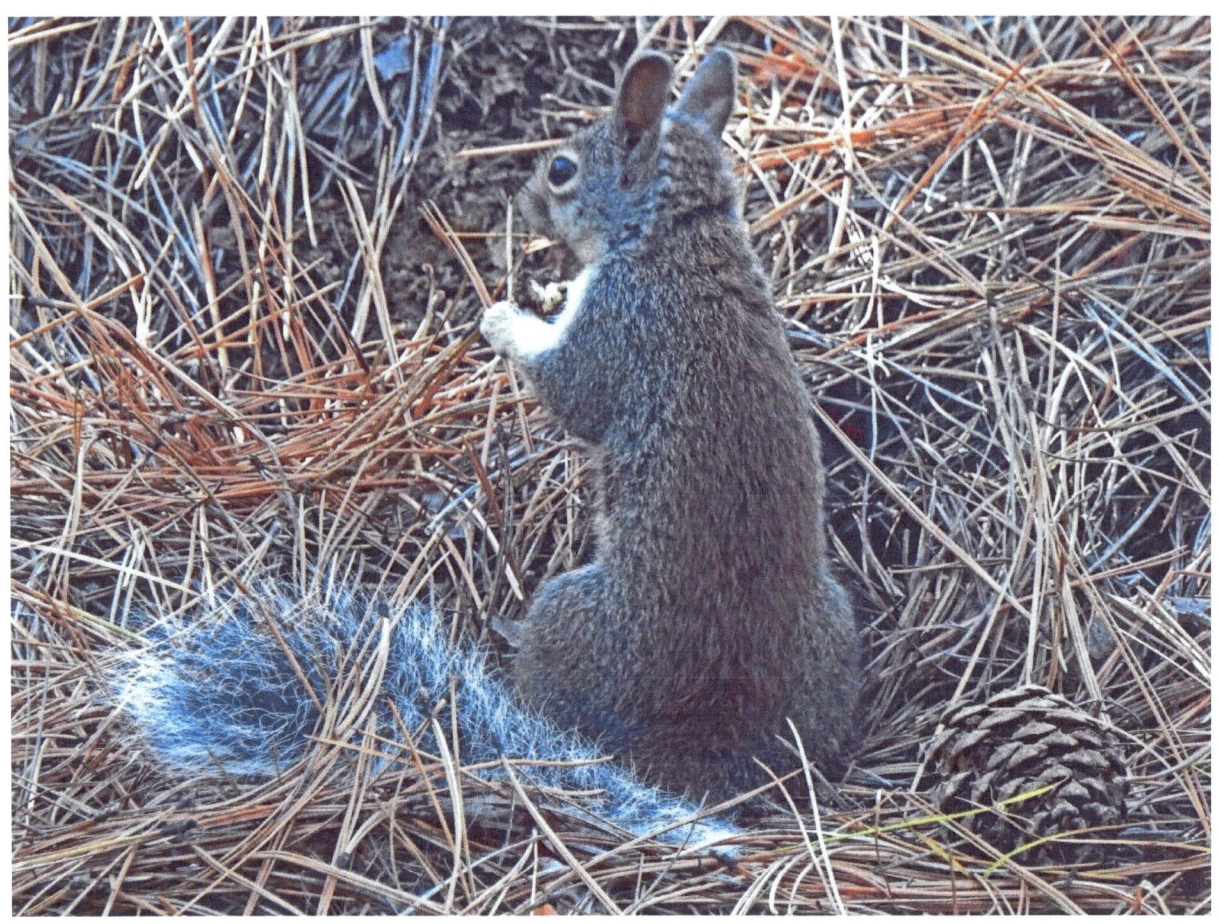

Note the Ponderosa Pine cone just behind the squirrel. In this picture, taken in mid-August, an Abert's Squirrel appears to be gathering fallen pine needles to line its nest. Females are the nest builders. Unlike birds that mainly use the nest for raising their young, squirrels prefer to sleep in their nest almost every night.

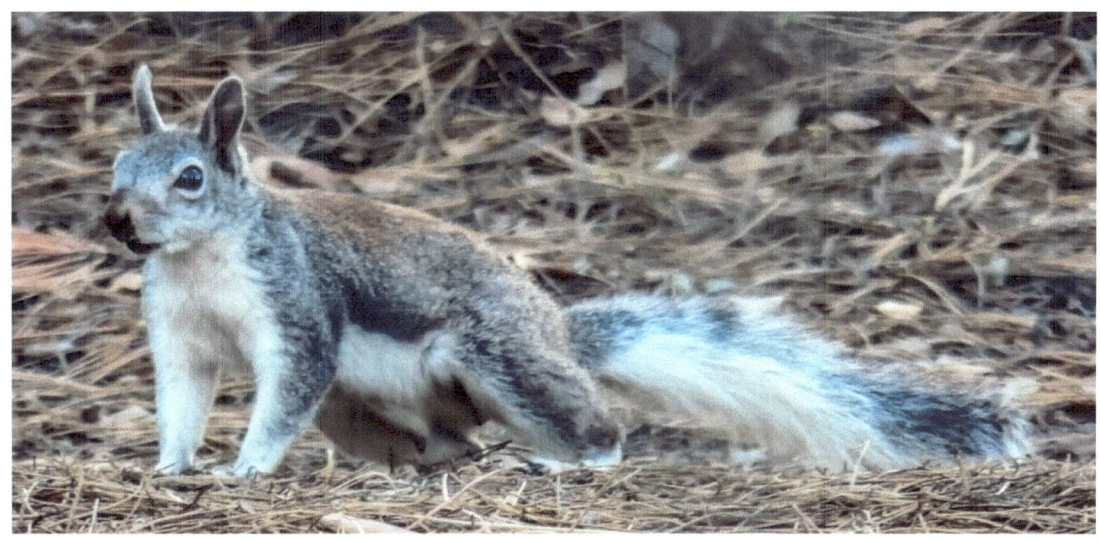

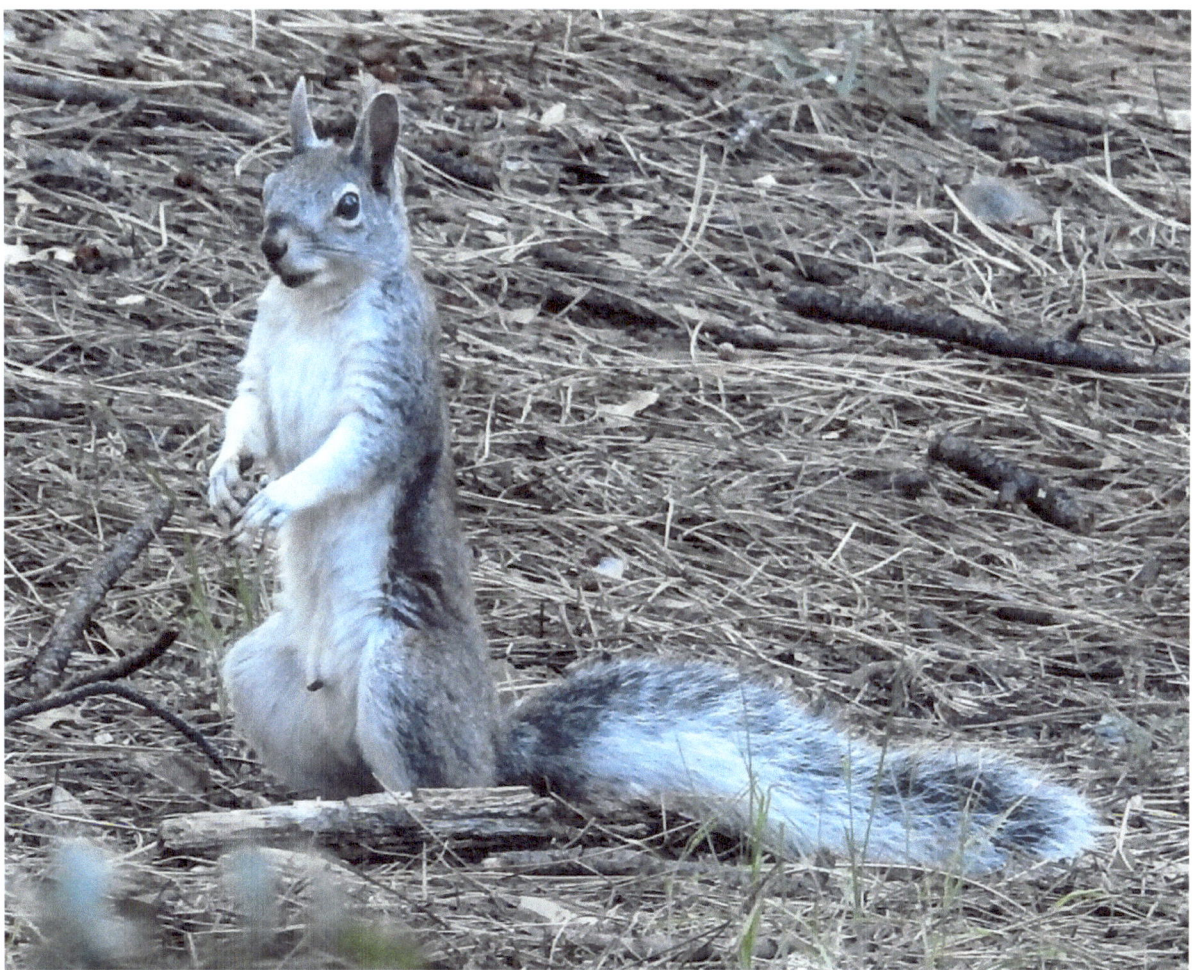

The top picture shows a lactating female and the lower one shows an aroused male. Breeding usually takes place in the summer months.

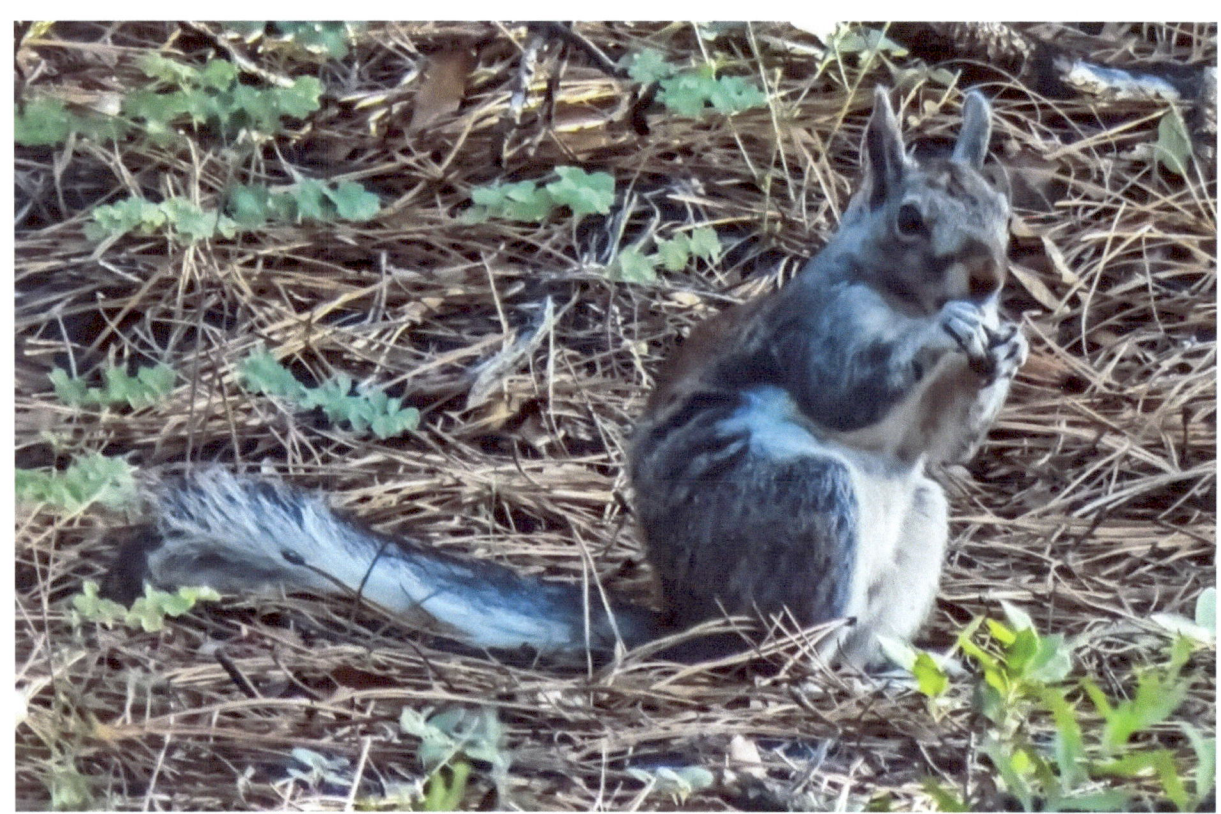

This picture was taken in mid-August. The rust-colored back of winter months is starting to develop. It is eating an acorn. Some Gambel's Oak leaves are in the background.

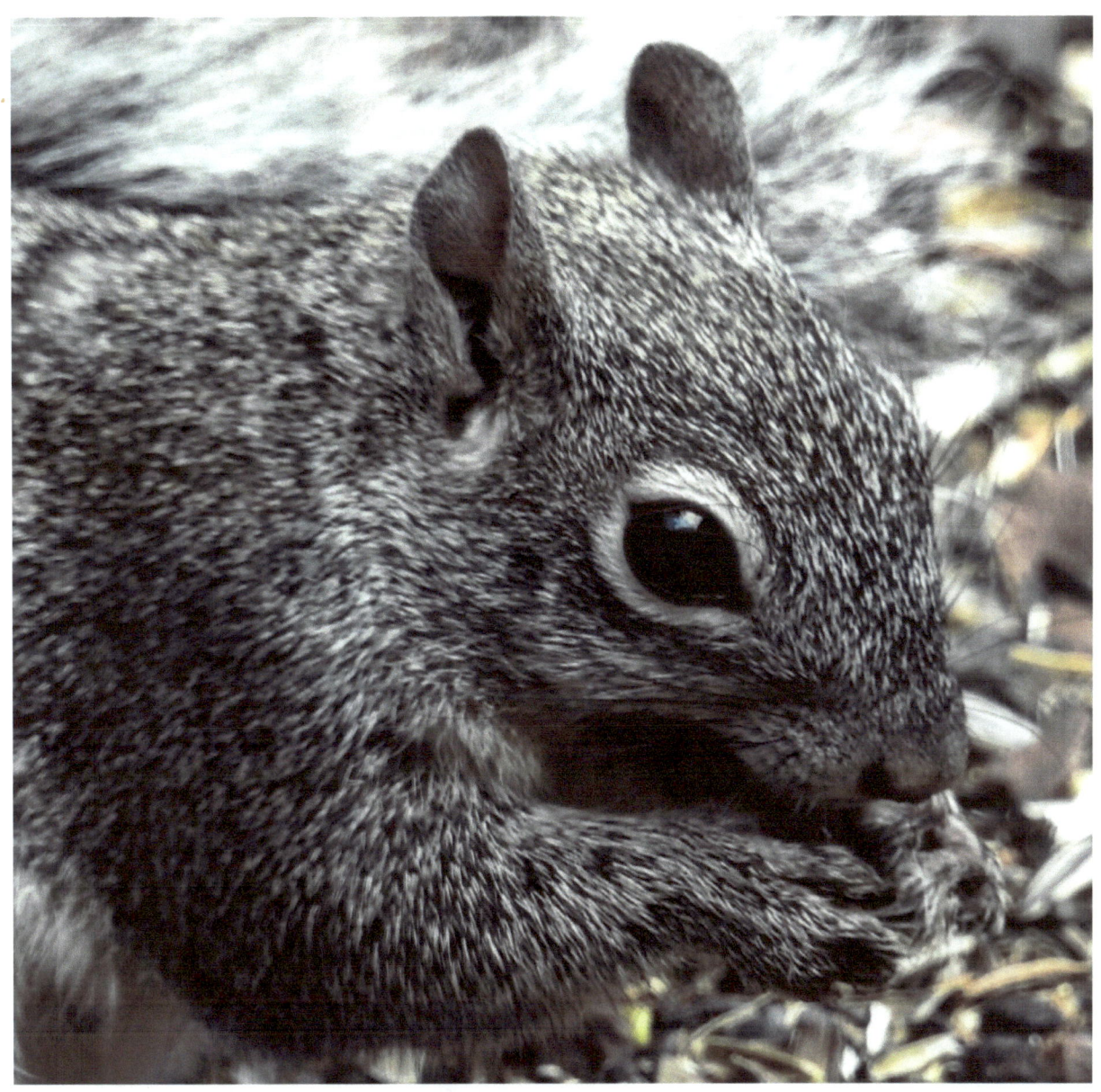

This picture is noteworthy for the details in the eye ring and the eye lashes of the Abert's Squirrel.

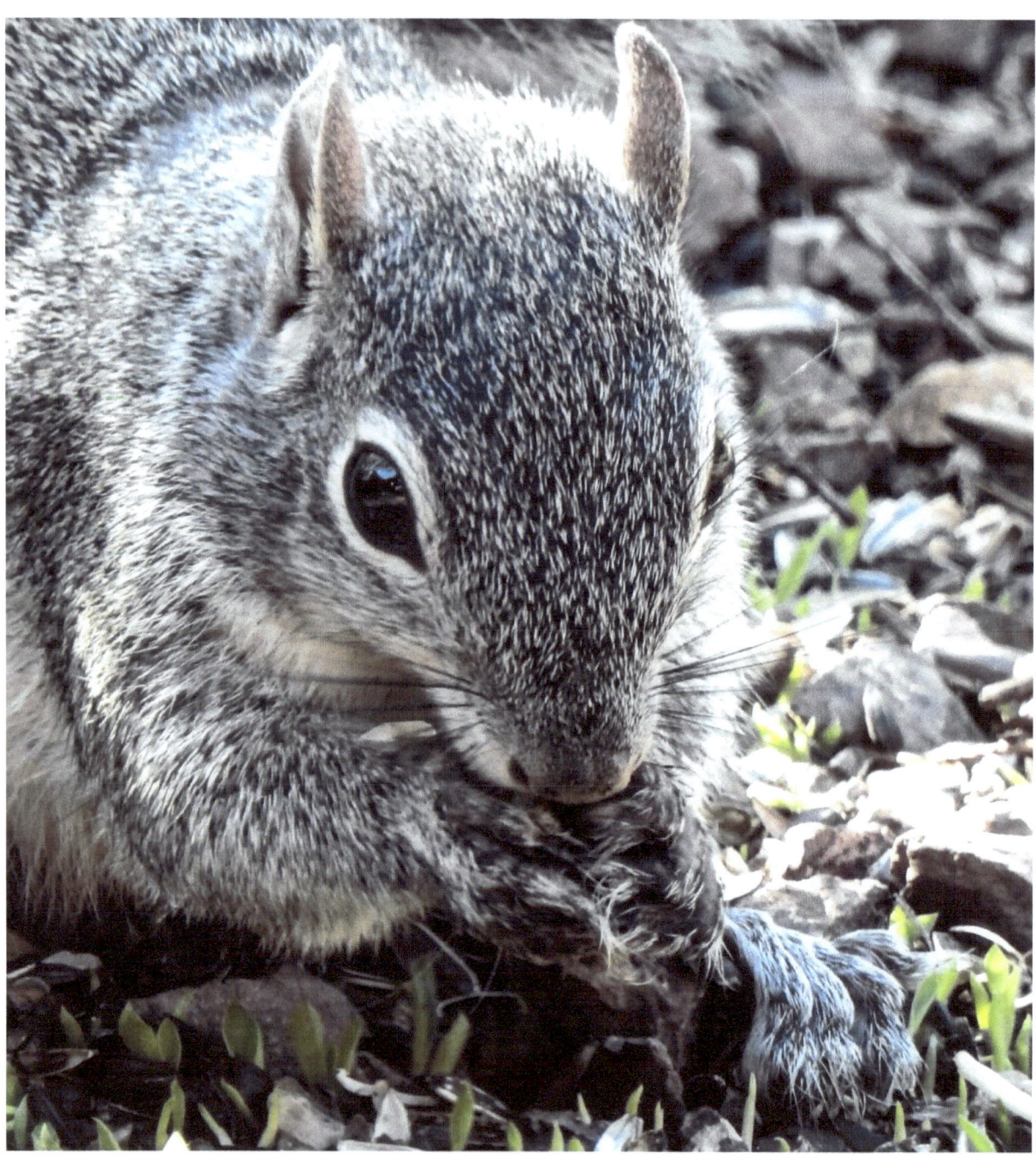

There are two noteworthy points in this picture. First, notice the number, the placement and length of the hairs in the mustache. Second, notice the placement of the hind feet particularly in the lower right of the picture. They are actually in front of the front feet. This allows for a powerful first leap if threatened.

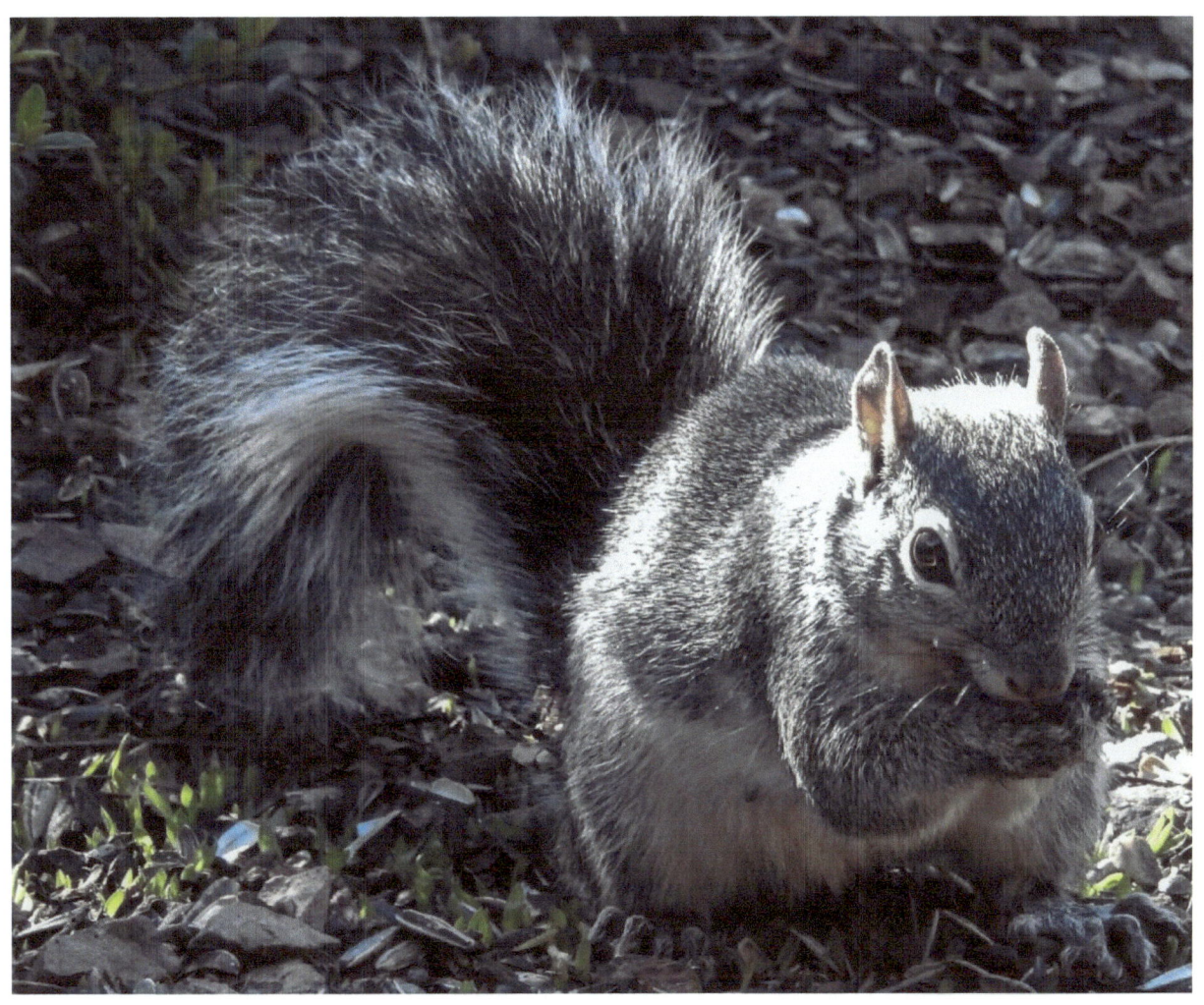

An Abert's Squirrel eats mostly vegetation. Since plant materials are not normally fast moving, they have no need for 3-dimensional vision. Having 3-D vision is usually found in fast-moving predators.

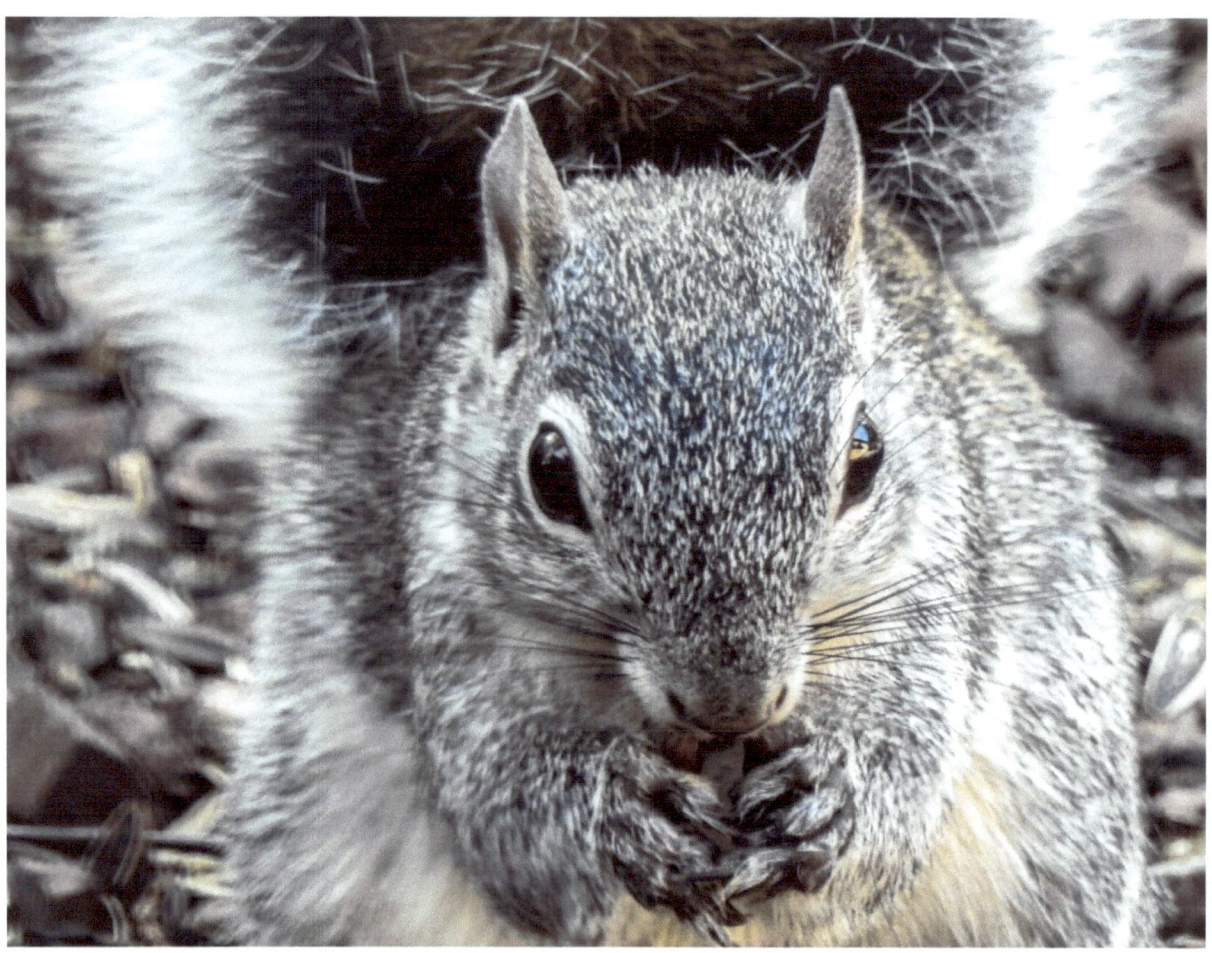

For Abert's Squirrels, the most important role vision plays is escaping from predators. Consequently, the eyes are set well to the sides of the head. The squirrel can even see threats from behind.

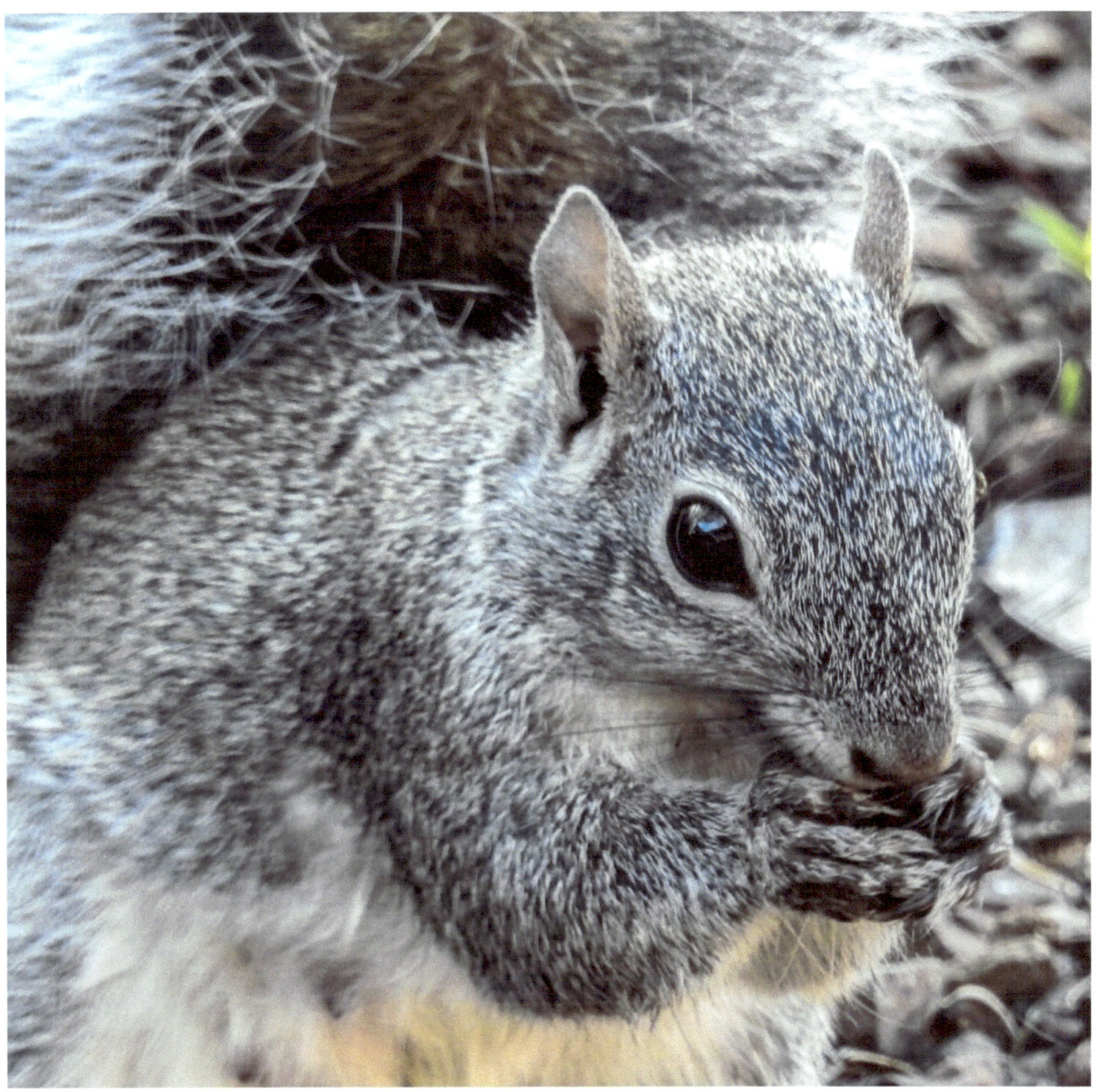

It is very faint, but if you look in the extreme lower right corner, you can see how the Abert's Squirrel places the claws of its hind feet while in a sitting position.

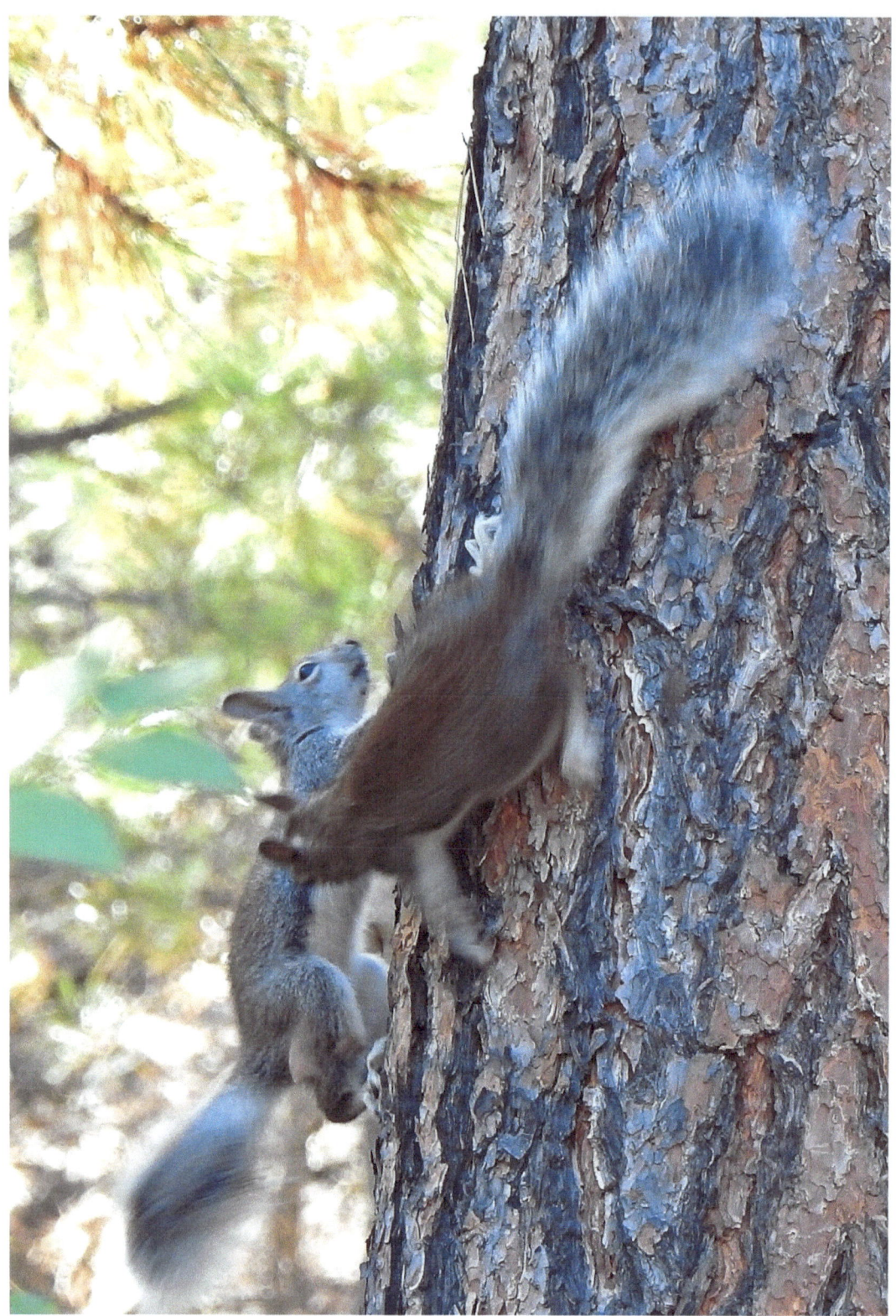

These two Abert's Squirrels were photographed at the same time in January as the lactating female shown earlier. She is probably the one on the right. They are on a Ponderosa Pine tree. A mature female and one of the offspring of her last litter are a common nest pairing during the winter for this species.

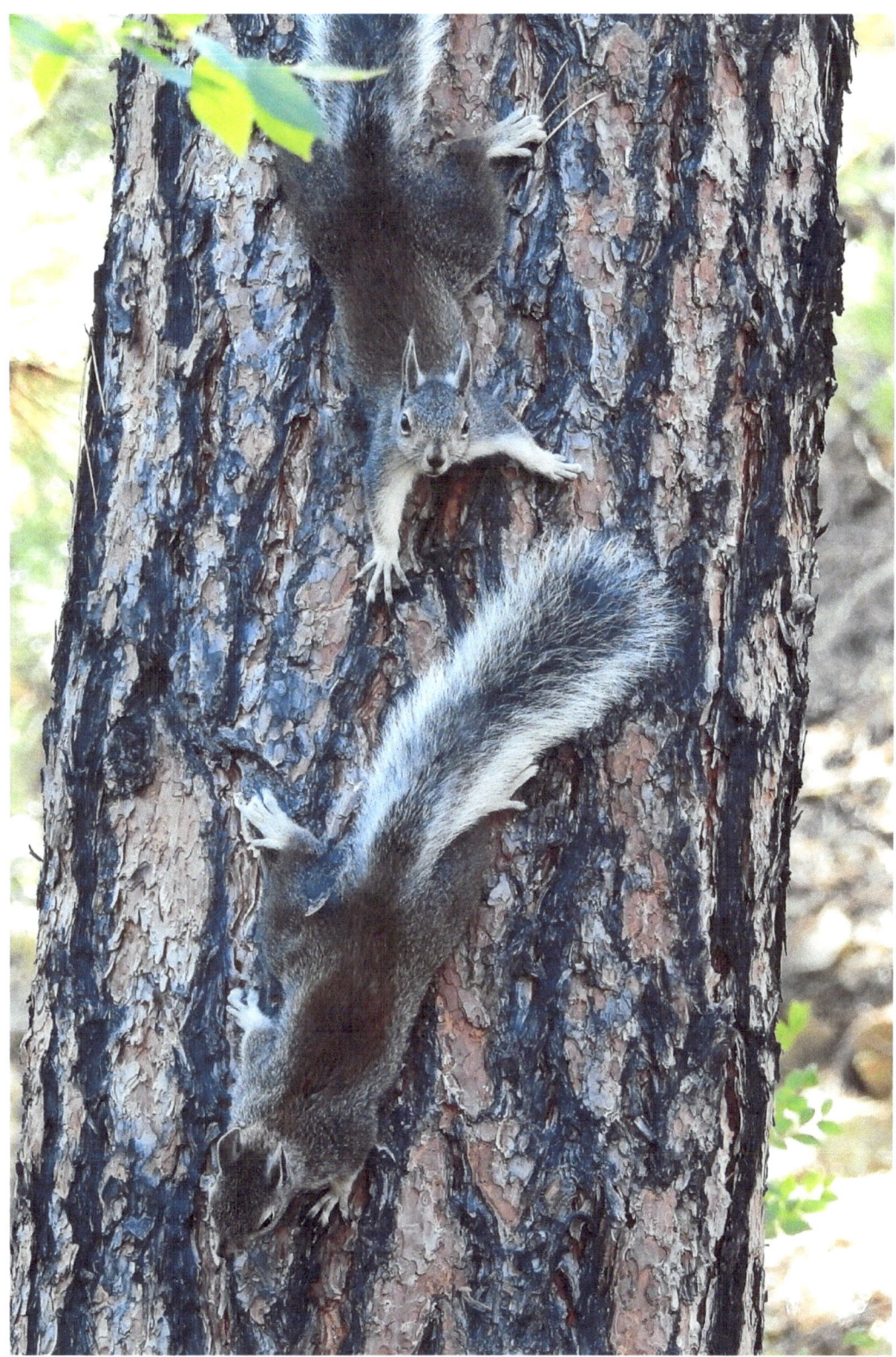

These are the same two squirrels shown on the previous page. The one higher up on the tree appears to have slightly longer ear tassels, so it is probably the female since she appeared to have a little more tassel showing in the previous picture.

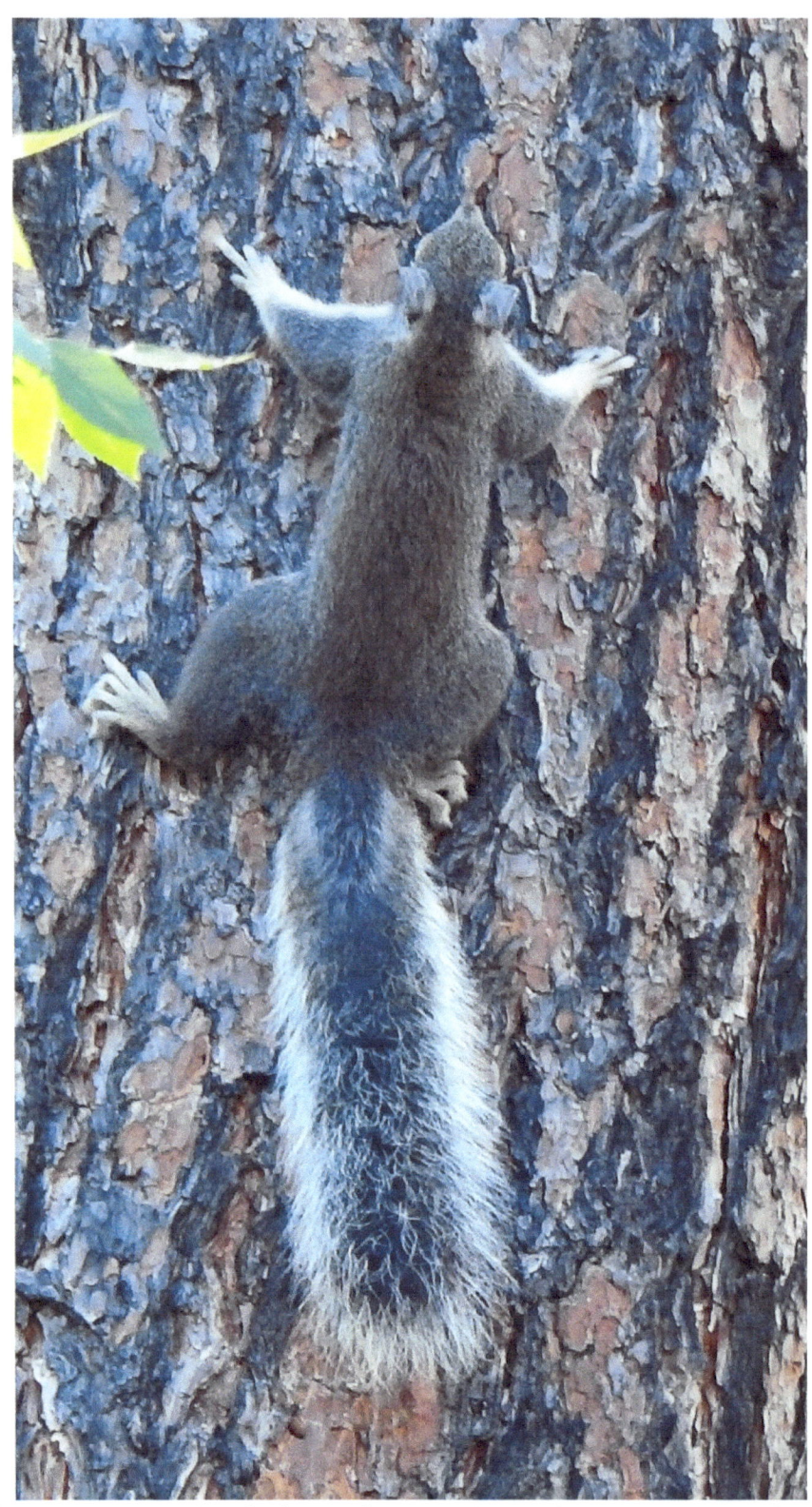

This is one of the same squirrels from the previous pictures except that here you can see its posture heading up the tree.

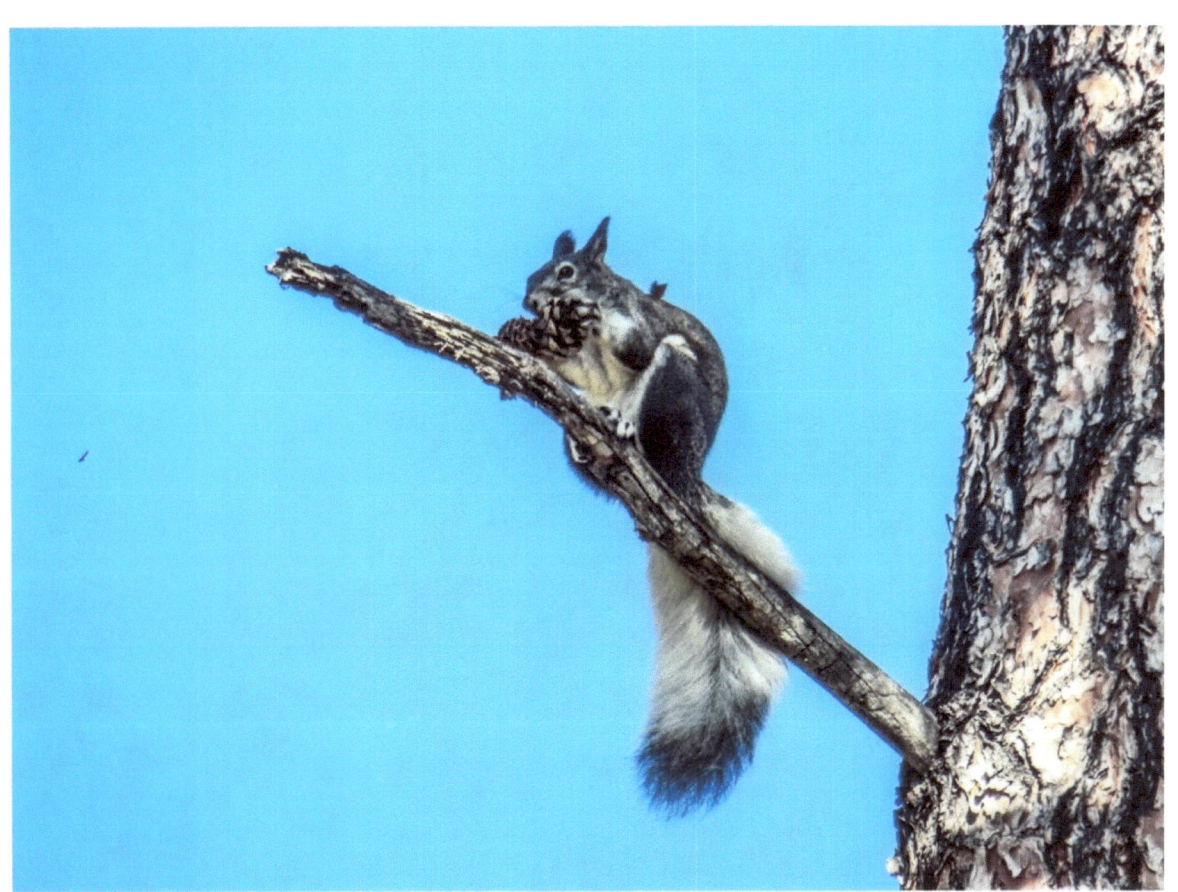

This squirrel is eating a Ponderosa Pine cone on the dead limb of a tree. Abert's Squirrels are able to make use of the water in their food to the extent that they rarely need to get a drink of water. Just above the squirrel's back, you can see a chip off the pine cone in mid-air. They flick the chips with a quick turn of their head. You might incorporate a chip in a more visible location in your picture.

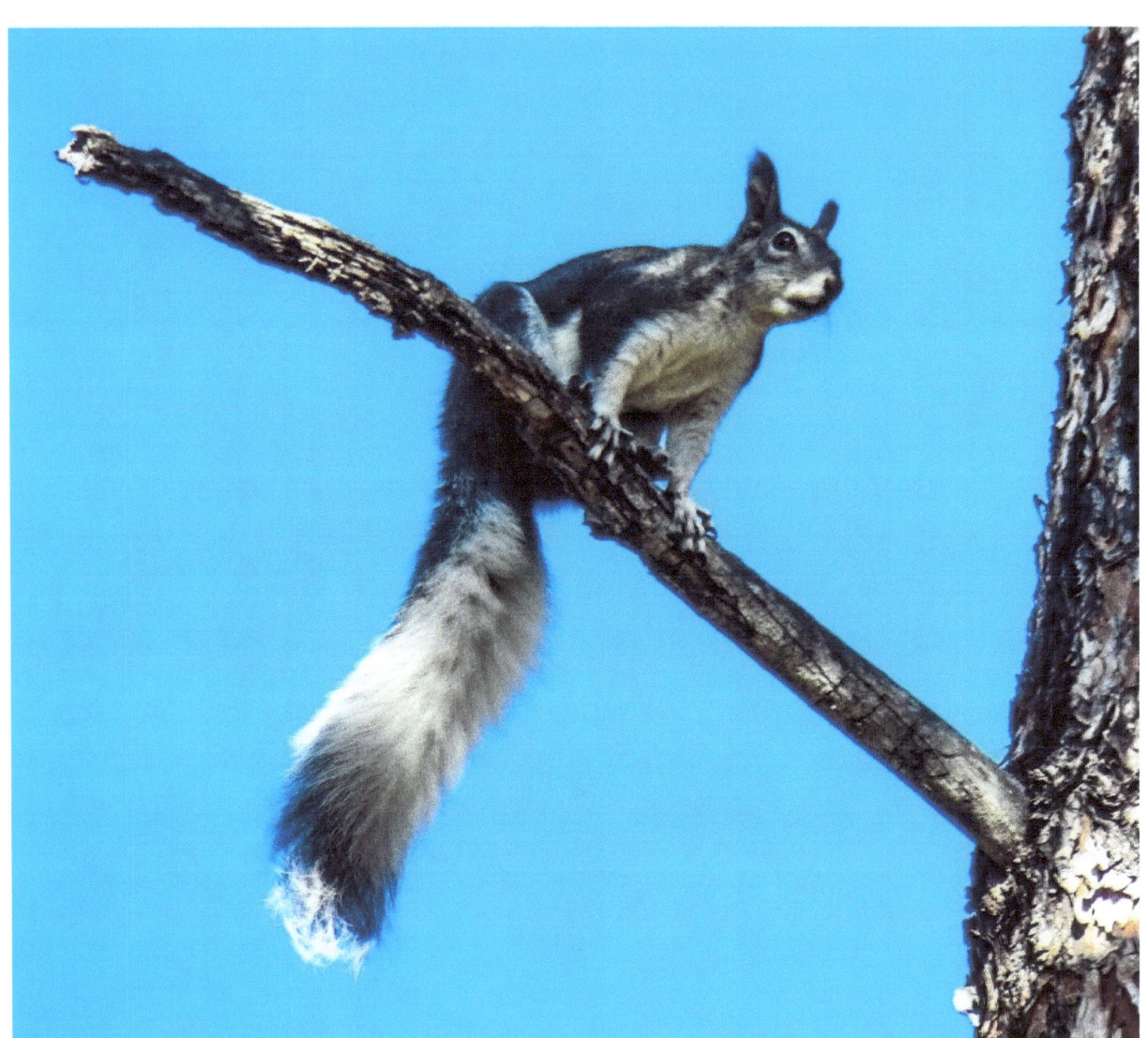

This is the same Abert's squirrel pictured on the previous page. It lost control of the pine cone and dropped it, so now it is about to jump from the dead limb in search of another food source. They rarely retrieve things that they drop.

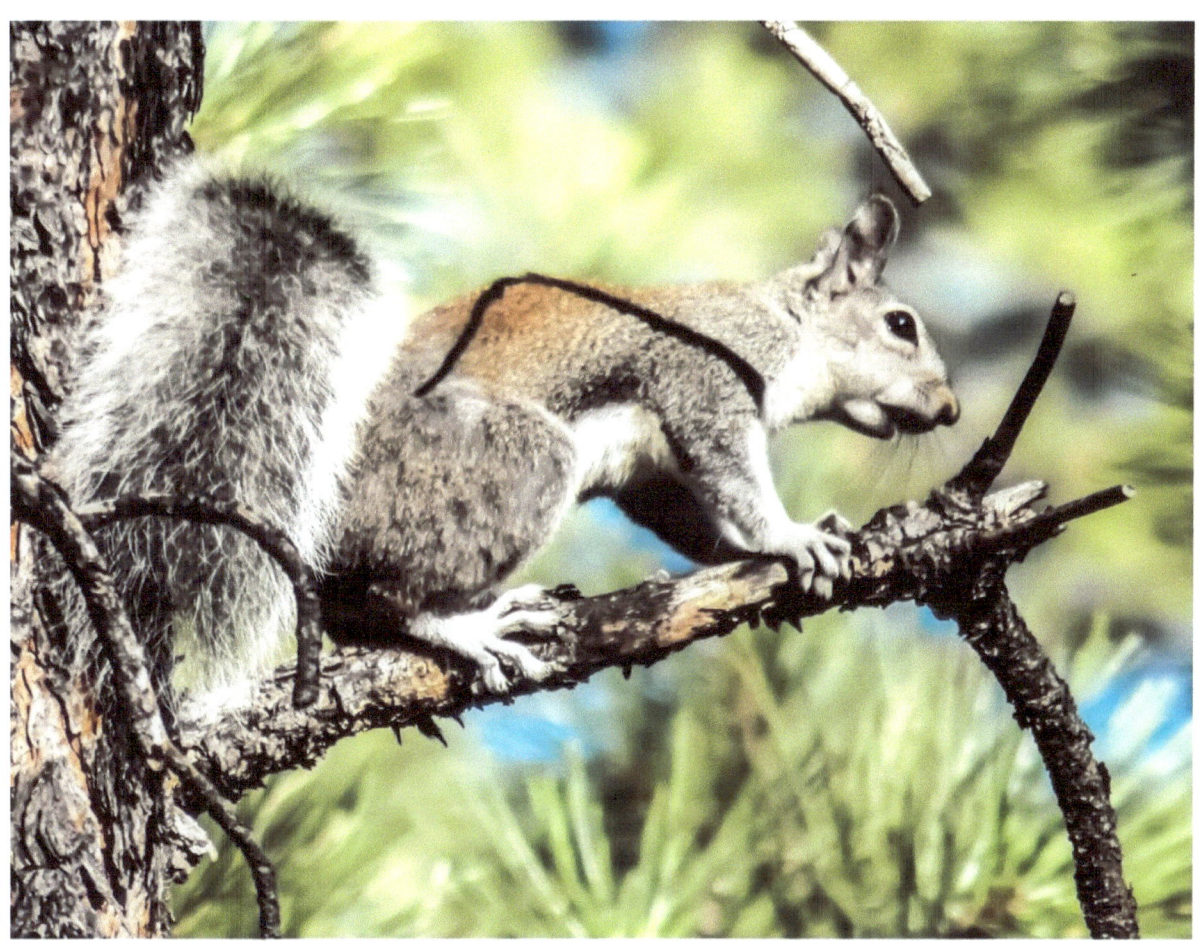

The dark stripe on the side of this squirrel is a shadow from an overhead twig. This illustrates how you could incorporate some extra details into your work.

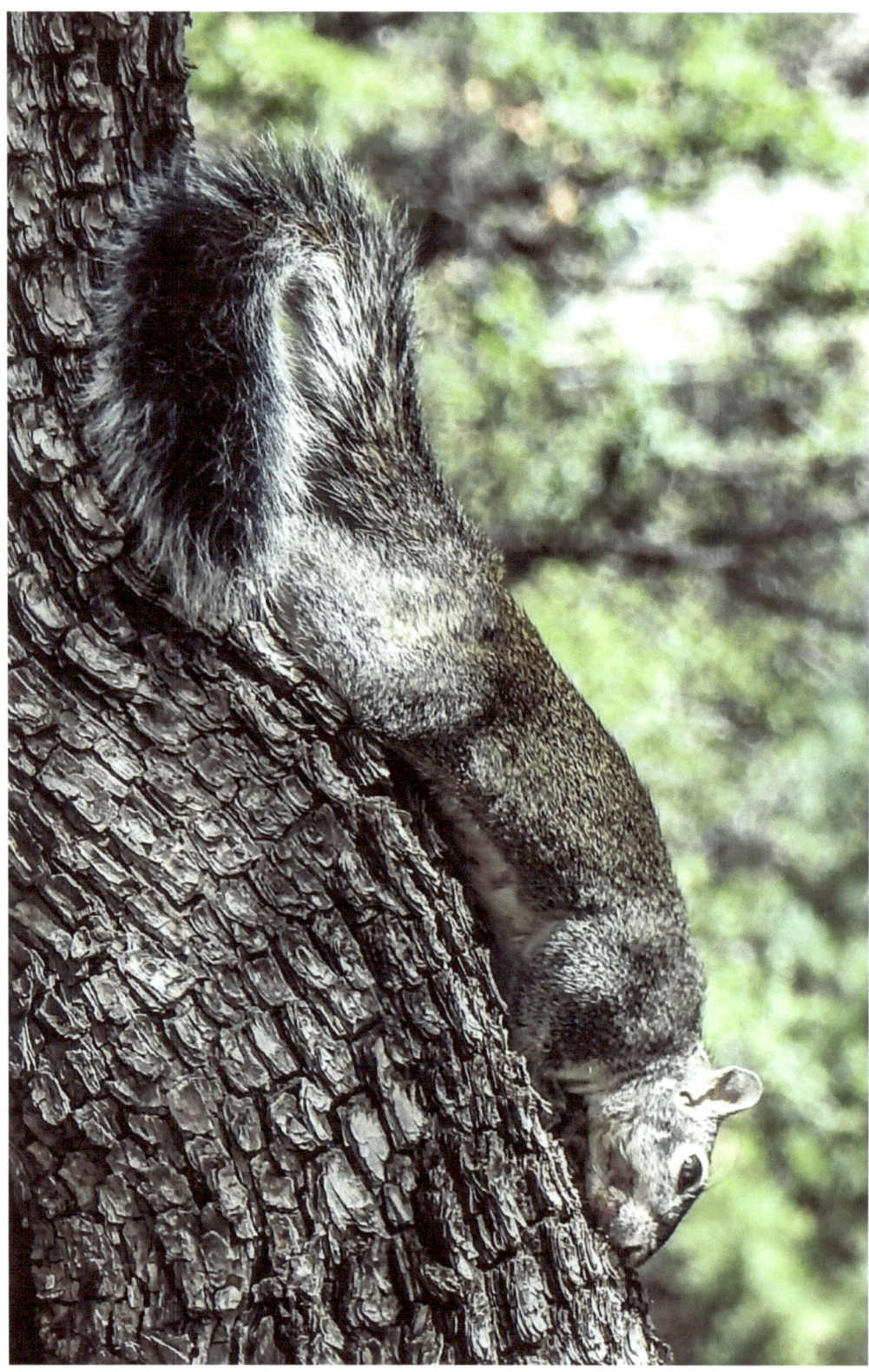

This Alligator Juniper tree is an unusual tree for an Abert's Squirrel. Generally these squirrels are found on Ponderosa Pines. However, in the central highlands of Arizona the two trees coexist in some places. If you use this pose, you might have a more acceptable picture if you change the bark to that of a Ponderosa.

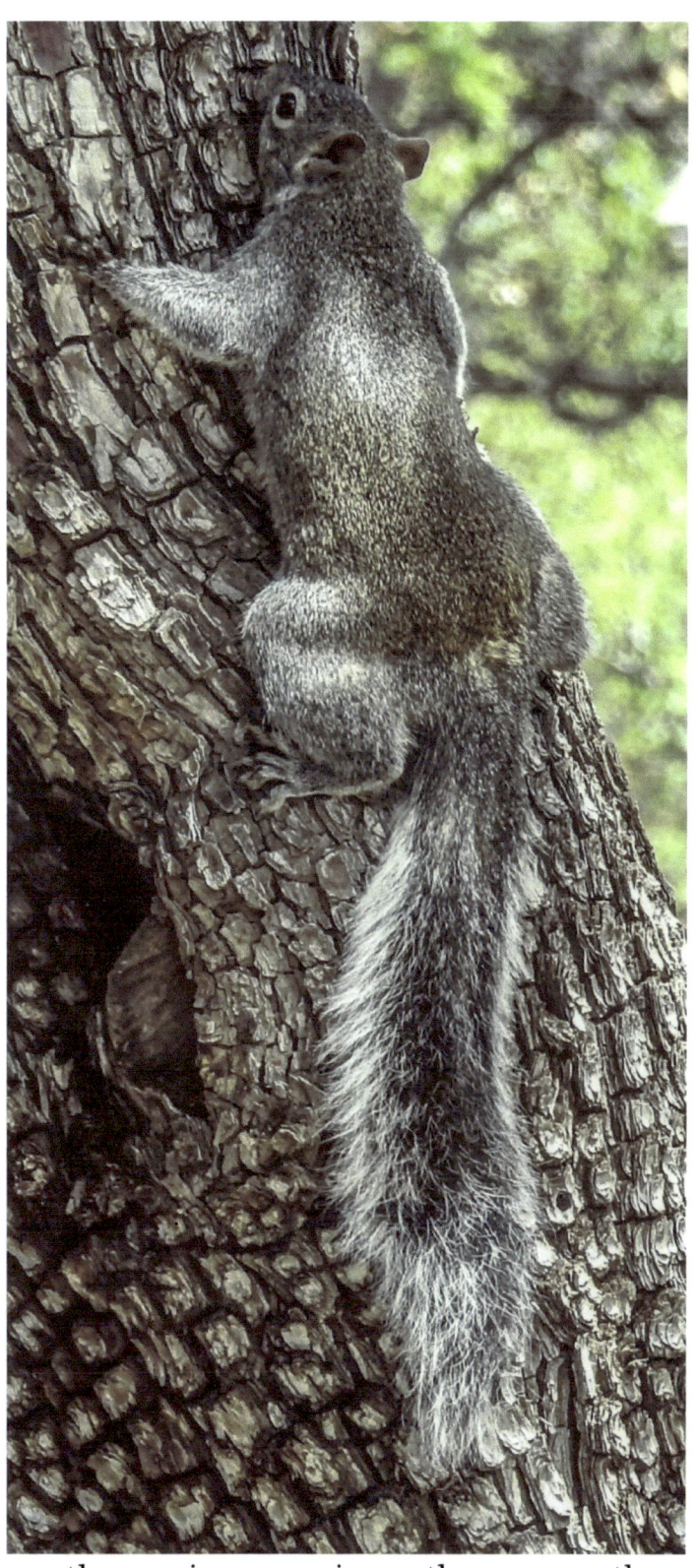

The same animal as on the previous page in another pose on the same tree.

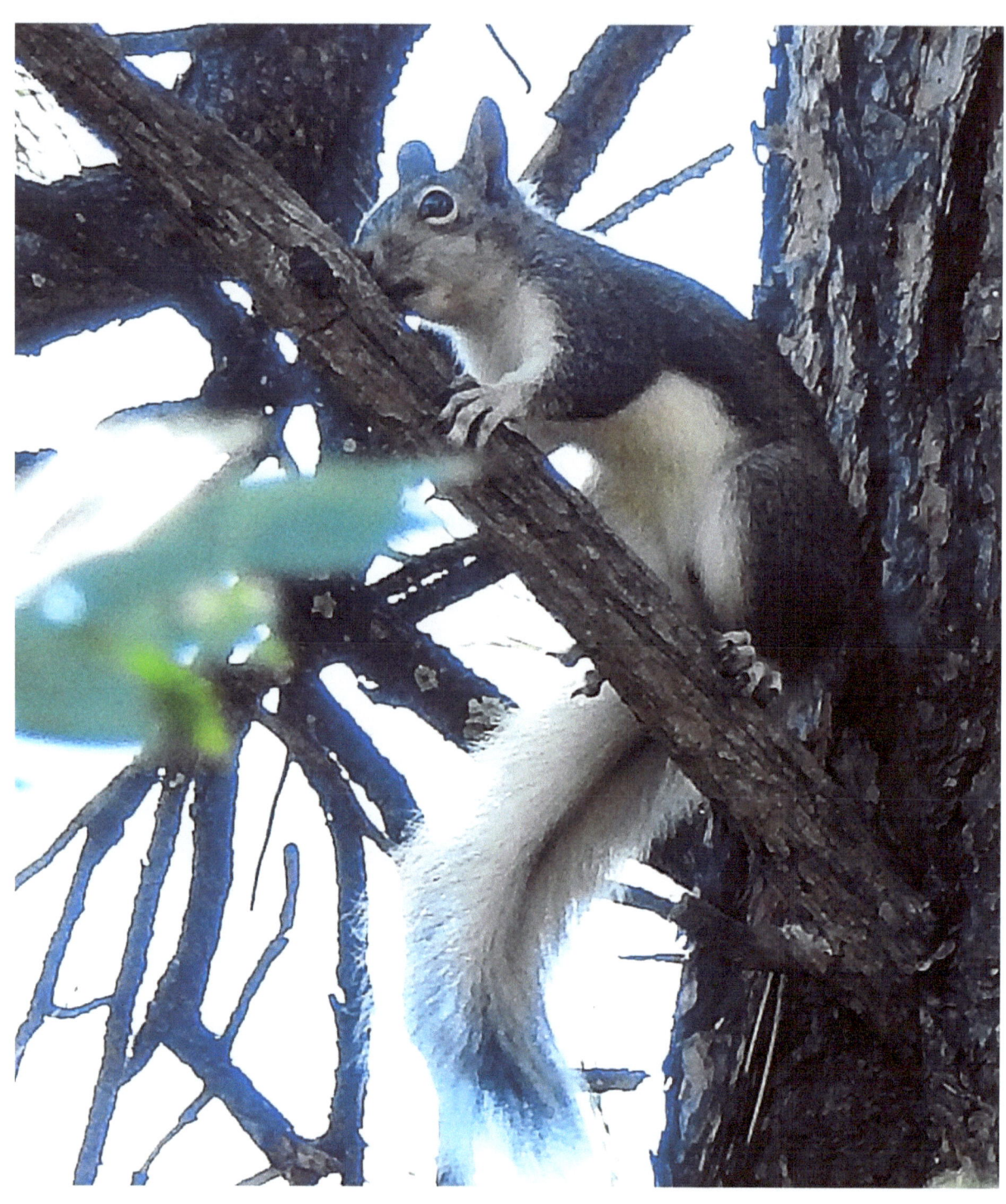

The parting shot. An Abert's Squirrel on a Ponderosa Pine limb in the springtime.

OTHER BOOKS BY AL LODWICK

The Homeschool Resource Series

Introduction to Birds

Gambel's Quail

Decisions for Preschoolers

The Preschooler's A-B-Cs of Nature

The Preschooler's Nature Book

Reference Photos For Nature Artists

Acorn Woodpeckers

Arizona Wildflowers

Bald Eagles

Cooper's Hawks

Double-crested Cormorants

Great Blue-Herons

Sedona: 50 Memorable Landscapes

Snakes and Lizards

Travel Guides

Grand Canyon National Park: The Roadtrip Guide

Highlights of The Highlands Center and Lynx Lake Area of Arizona: A Naturalist's View

Biblical

The Creation Story: King James Version with Photographs

Pharmacy Practice

Expand Your Pharmacy Practice: Become an Expert Witness or Litigation Consultant

Novel With Scott Mies

Murder or Pestle